The Little Book of Lonelyhearts

The Little Book of Lonelyhearts

By

Del Cullen
Hannah Patterson
Howard Seal
Paul Matthew Thompson

This edition published in 2008 by Oldcastle Book
PO Box 394, Harpenden, Herts, AL5 1XJ
www.oldcastlebooks.com

A CIP catalogue record for this book is available from the British Library.

EAN 978-1-84243-274-7

2 4 6 8 10 9 7 5 3 1

Printed and bound by SNP Lefung Printers (Shenzen) Co Ltd, China

For hopeless romantics everywhere

This is a guide intended to assist you on your path to true love

Feel free to use any of the suggestions listed in this book

But ignore the Lonelyhearts rules at your peril

There are lots of sad, lonely bastards out there, but plenty of nice people too

Good luck and don't lose heart

MEN
SEEKING
W♥MEN

ARCHAEOLOGIST SEEKS
TO UNEARTH TRUE LOVE
AGE NO BARRIER

PUSSY GALORE
Lion-tamer seeks Burmese sex kitten
Big whip

single parent seeks single parent for babysitting

CATCH OF THE DAY
CORNISH FISHERMAN SEEKS LIKE-MINDED HOOKER

No old trouts

Farmer aged 52 wishes to meet unmarried woman in early 40s who owns a tractor. Please send photo of tractor.

ON THE MARKET

**ESTATE AGENT, 24, SEEKS GIRL NEXT DOOR
(IDEALLY WITH SOUTH FACING GARDEN)**

LIGHT MY FIRE!
ARSONIST SEEKS PERFECT MATCH

Handsome graduate, 31, seeks intelligent, affectionate and sensual Sagittarius to share the most perfect love this strange and beautiful world has ever seen.

O.N.O

LARGE BAPS?
STUD MUFFIN SEEKS CRUMPET

Gym knickers: PE teacher seeks willing pupil for fun and games (Bring your own towel)

missed connection   m4w

lime st
station, platform 11
u smiled
as u dialled
a number
o
i was in heaven :-)
i followed, but u and ur
petite
feet
were 2 quick 4 me

LATE WITHDRAWAL!

**RICH BANKER – 57 – URGENTLY SEEKS FOURTH WIFE
WEDDING ON SATURDAY**

~

LOVE JOY
ANTIQUES DEALER SEEKS PRICELESS
TREASURE FOR RESTORATION
NO FAKES

~

NAPPY FETISH
Big baby seeks maternal woman to change him

Sad Twat Seeks Bird

READING BETWEEN THE LINES

Attractive	**Vain**
Fairly Attractive	**Fairly Ugly**
Bubbly	**Irritating**
Romantic	**Expensive**
Curvy	**Fat**
Cuddly	**Really Fat**

Curvaceous	**Fat and Posh**
Petite	**Anorexic**
Voluptuous	**Big Tits**
Well-Built	**Small Penis**
Hunky	**Small Brain**
Spontaneous	**Promiscuous**
Happy Go Lucky	**Easy**

W♥MEN
SEEKING
MEN

RAISA LEGOVA: **RUSSIAN GYMNAST SEEKS SUPPLE PARTNER FOR QUICK FLING**

U-BEND
BORED HOUSEWIFE NEEDS
EXPERIENCED PLUMBER (21-29)
MORNINGS ONLY

Saturday. Nadia and Colin's fancy dress party.

I was the Cher lookalike.
I think you were Barry Manilow.
You sat on my vol-au-vent and
my world stopped turning.

Could it be Magic?

ORIENT EXPRESS
MATURE THAI LADY SEEKS
TRAVELLING COMPANION
GOES LIKE A TRAIN

NAKED GUN?

FARNHAM FEMME FATALE SEEKS PRIVATE DICK FOR HIRE

English Rose
Ideal for Bedding

MIDDLE
AGED
OPTICIAN
SEEKS
GOOD
LOOKING
SHORT
SIGHTED
MAN

CUCKOO!
**HOMESICK SWISS MISS SEEKS
MAN WITH BIG CLOCK
NO TIMEWASTERS**

COME-BYE!
LITTLE BO PEEP SEEKS
ONE MAN AND HIS DOG

EYE CANDY

sweetie seeks sugar daddy.
you get Viagra. i get your money

Sun Sep 09

Wayward blonde seeks hairdresser for LTR (Essex)

GONE TO SEED!

**DIVORCEE, 44, SEEKS VERSATILE
LANDSCAPE GARDENER
TO TRIM HER BUSH**

Busy professional seeks Perfect Man. Film star looks essential. Athletic build. MENSA IQ. Send sperm to PO Box 45302.

COME DANCING!

EASTBOURNE LADY, 89, SEEKS
WILLING PARTNER FOR LAST WALTZ.
TUESDAYS AND THURSDAYS.

WILL CONSIDER SEX NEARER THE TIME

£££

Sharon. Escort. No dinner required.

READING BETWEEN THE LINES

WLTM	**Would Like To Marry**
GSOH	**Grating Sense of Humour**
Mysterious	**Married**
Adventurous	**Perverted**
Cultured	**Pretentious**
Sun Seeker	**Fake Tan**

Sensitive	**Wet**
Energetic	**Hyperactive**
Chatty	**Annoying**
Caring	**Clingy**
Vivacious	**Tiring**
Sentimental Dreamer	**Lazy Bastard**
Quirky	**Wears a Hat**

MEN
SEEKING
MEN

CHUBBY CHASER!
FAT BLOKE SEEKS BIG BEAR FOR FLABBY FUN

Distinguished gent, 63, retired public school master,
WLTM attractive younger man for 1-2-1.
PLEASE no more hustlers.

BUCKING BRONCO

ESSEX COWBOY SEEKS STALLION
FOR BARE BACK RIDES
(spurs provided)

Top man seeks bottom

WIND SURFER SEEKS SEAMAN
FOR WATER SPORTS

SPLASH ME!

dancing queen seeks dj for bj

WARDBROBE ASSISTANT SEEKS STRAIGHT
ACTING GAFFER WITH BIG HANGERS

COME OUT OF THE CLOSET NANCY!

GAY MEN EVERYWHERE
JESUS STILL LOVES YOU

my old man? teenage twink seeks father figure

READING BETWEEN THE LINES

Genuine	**False**
Cheeky	**Rude**
Neat	**Anal**
Stylish	**Fashion-Victim**
Groovy	**Old Hippie**
Bisexual	**Greedy**

Teetotal	**Recovering Alcoholic**
Bon Viveur!	**Drunken Old Lush**
Sensitive	**Paranoid**
Wacky	**Weird**
Student	**Skint & Spotty**
Intellectual	**Smart Arse**
Versatile	**Takes it up the Arse**

Feet first
Dyslexic chiropodist – 28 – seeks sole mate

Foxy Fraulein

LANGUAGE TRANSLATOR,
STRASBOURG, SEEKS SIMILAR
FOR BILINGUAL CUNNILINGUAL

Where have all the flowers gone?
'Silently, she laid her down on sumptuous
silken pillows; her lips parting, her breasts
glistening. This was the moment she had
waited for, longed for, yearned for...'

Romantic novelist seeks muse for happy ending.

And literary agent.

SAPPHIC SISTERS

VENUS
SEEKS
APHRODITE
FOR
LOVE-IN

DEEP SEA DIVER SEEKS PEARL
Hidden depths

**BIKE DYKE SEEKS GREASE MONKEY
FOR LUBE JOB**

EASY RIDER!

Calling the women of Wales!
It's that time again!
The Llandudno Lesbian Librarians are about
to Mount Snowdon!
Plenty of space still available!

READING BETWEEN THE LINES

Northern Soul	**Moaner**
Sensible Scot	**Stingy Moaner**
Chirpy Cockney	**Rough Minger**
Cheeky Scouser	**Petty Thief**
Ladies' Man	**Closet Homosexual**
Man's Man	**Closet Homosexual**

Straight Acting	**Camp after a Few Drinks**
Party Animal	**Cocaine Addict**
Film Buff	**Difficult Glasses**
Enjoys Travel	**Can't Commit**
New to Area	**Just Out of Prison**
All Calls Answered	**Desperate**
Committed	**Bunny Boiler**

CASUAL ENCOUNTERS

Schizophrenic seeks Siamese twins for double-trouble

DOGGING!
Barking swingers seek like-minded couples
for outdoor fun in Epping Forest

NYMPHOMANIAC NEEDS SEX.
Really not fussy.

**Buddhist
Monkey in former life
Seeks Nirvana**

Romantic Suffolk lady. First class

degree in ceramics. Collects Toby

jugs, with a passion for Fuc-

hsias, Beethoven and wal-

king outdoors in the rain.

Serious applicants should only read lines 1, 3 & 5

Short man seeks dwarf to talk
down to.
No trolls.

TRANSVESTITE SEEKS BLOUSY LADY WITH TOLERANT ATTITUDE AND SIZE 9 SHOES

Chronic agoraphobic needs mail order pornography

Chronic claustrophobic needs to get out more

Del, 29, seeks lifeboat

HEARING-IMPAIRED TROMBONIST SEEKS SYMPATHETIC PARTNER. DON'T LET A CRY FOR HELP FALL ON DEAF EARS

Happinessisnowhere

Fat depressive seeks an end.

READING BETWEEN THE LINES

Keen Gardener	**Rough Hands**
Keen Walker	**Unemployed**
Company Director	**Works from a Bedroom**
Salt of the Earth	**Common**
Free Spirit	**No Fixed Abode**
Unlucky in Love	**Three Times Divorced**

Deep Thinker	**Moody**
Frustrated Poet	**Suicidal**
Female Vegan	**Hairy Armpits**
Shirley Valentine	**Middle Aged Frump**
Laid Back Philosopher	**Paraplegic**
Good with Kids	**Paedophile**
God's Messenger	**Serial Killer**

You've found your date

Hardest part over

But plenty could still go wrong…

GOLDEN RULE NUMBER ONE

<u>Never</u> get drunk on a first date

GOLDEN RULE NUMBER TWO

<u>Never</u> have sex on a first date

(unless you ignore the first rule and get drunk)

GOLDEN RULE NUMBER THREE

Eye contact is everything

(unless your date is blind)

GOLDEN RULE NUMBER FOUR

Don't get bogged down with compatible star signs

(a shag's a shag, whether they're Libra or Taurus)

GOLDEN RULE NUMBER FIVE

Always phone a friend to let them know
where you are

(but never invite them to join you)

GOLDEN RULE NUMBER SIX

Never talk about your ex

(even if they're sitting at the next table with
your best friend)

GOLDEN RULE NUMBER SEVEN

Don't flirt with the waiter

(unless he's single, available and better looking
than your date)

GOLDEN RULE NUMBER EIGHT

Doner kebabs are not an aphrodisiac

GOLDEN RULE NUMBER NINE

Bald men are rumoured to be more virile

(but they're still bald)